NO NEED TO RUN

Take a Stand

Dr. Marci Tilghman-Bryant

No Need to Run "Take a Stand"
By Dr. Marci Tilghman-Bryant

Cover Designed by Leroy Grayson
Published by Jazzy Kitty Publications
Logo Designed by Justin Ackerman
Editor: Anelda L. Attaway

© 2023 Dr. Marci Tilghman-Bryant
ISBN 978-1-954425-81-1
Library of Congress Control Number: 2023913302

ACKNOWLEDGMENTS

To my entire BVT Outreach family, including Deacon Clarence E. Tilghman Sr. Their support has been awesome and the encouragement I received has helped me keep moving forward doing what I love...writing to entertain, improve and change lives.

TABLE OF CONTENTS

INTRODUCTION

Hebrews 12:1-7 (NKJV)

You're running!

Have you ever stopped long enough to ask yourself why? This book has found its way into your hand because your soul's cry has been heard, not by man, but by the Spirit. It wants you to stop running! Your soul is crying out for rest. Peace be still! Even champions must face the truth that one day it's time to slow the pace and remove themselves from the race and refrain from the constant activity.

Resting is not just the simple activity of slowing down, sitting, or lying down. True rest is trust!

Who do you trust? What do you have faith in? When do you find yourself on the brink of self-doubt? Where are you emotionally and mentally in times of great trials and stressful moments? Why do you react the way you do?

Please don't walk away from this or put this book down until you have examined the first few pages of its content. If these words do not speak to your inner man, put it back on the shelf and keep running. But if you find these inspired words tugging at your core, you must follow this path until you cross the finish line with your whole soul intact, at rest, and at peace.

Defining the Runner

We are all runners. Some of us run from, some of us run to, some of us run around, some of us run away. But make no mistake, we all run. We all are running for different reasons, but not all of us cross the finish line. Some of us never discover why we are running, so we just keep up the mundane activity until we wear ourselves out. This is a sad fate to be engaged in a movement that affects your life, yet you don't know why; you just keep moving with no rhyme or reason for your behavior.

Another sad thing is this; some of us get tired and just stop along the journey, finding ourselves filled with emptiness. We know we can't keep going, but we are agitated at keeping still, so when we keep still, it is because there is no physical strength left; the outward man is still, but the inner man is not at rest. On the inside, we are still churning and burning but getting nowhere.

Running signifies action or movement. It's built into our DNA. The reasons we run are many. The reasons we stop are many. But today is your day of self-discovery. Today you will learn what category you fall into and why.

The "From" Runner

First, let me speak to the persons who are running FROM. You will find a large number of people in this group. People run from responsibility; they have never quite learned how to assume it or deal with it in their everyday life. So, it becomes easier for them to pawn it off on someone else's plate. This group runs from confrontation; facing the challenge of someone else's position that differs from their own causes them great distress. They haven't learned to deal with opposition. They are not secure within themselves.

This group also runs from disappointment and failure. They have never developed the fortitude to face up to their inadequacies or the inadequacies of others. They have not yet given themselves over to the strengthening of their human resolve. This group runs from commitment. Commitment requires sacrifice. They have never learned to share, so they remain locked in a selfish prison of which they have disguised as "live and let live!"

Additionally, this group runs from the inevitable, like growing old. Our society is so immersed with "image consciousness," or the outer appearance, that billions of dollars are spent on cosmetics, surgery, designer clothing, even the type of car we drive etc. This group lives in such denial. While they say with their mouths that age is only a number or that you are only as old as you feel, they often miss warning signs that would alert them of impending danger to their health or well-being. Doctors and specialists are telling patients every day, "If you had followed up when the symptoms first occurred," "If you had come in sooner and the problem had been diagnosed earlier," "If only you hadn't ignored the side effects of this particular drug and discontinued its use"…you name it, the list goes on.

You will also find in this group people who run from loneliness. They build up so much work and busy activities in their lifestyle that there is little to no time for relaxation, vacation, alone time, reflection, or for just being still. They have not even learned to be comfortable with who they are. They just work and sleep. They often eat on the run. Their lives are full of people, places, and things, but empty when they come to wherever they call home. So, for them, they have to be so tired when they enter into that space that all that comes to them is the welcoming onset of sleep. Some even find alcohol as a gentle persuasion to lull the senses to numbness until the next conscious moment and the cycle begins again.

They run from embarrassment. Oh, the utter shame of it all to face up to one's ignorance. Truly this individual has not learned to look at the lighter side of life and laughter. Laughter is like medicine. It can turn an awkward situation into a wonderful bonding and what would have been devastating just melts away into nothingness. But some don't find this balance; they run instead.

Do you find yourself in any one or two or more of these descriptions? Don't fret; there is hope. There are answers and solutions to this type of runner. The question is simply this...do you want to stop running from???

The "To" Runner

Secondly, there is a group that runs "to"

These people are always chasing the next shadow of possibility. They have no specific vision, but they believe in sheer optimism. "If I can just do this or that, this or that will happen. If it doesn't happen on this track, I will simply move to another track; I will move until it finally hits!" They are primarily money-motivated or love motivated (not the agape type of love, but the sensual kind, eros). They look for one, the money, or the other, eros, in all the wrong places. The wrong places can be identified as "get rich quick" schemes or the person who walks into their lives with a hidden agenda, which usually causes them a great deal of pain when the so-called relationship ends. Instead of stopping to evaluate where it all went wrong, this person just keeps moving toward the next opportunity. And at best, they only enjoy a temporary state of bliss. Yes, even though the bliss is fleeting, and just having experienced a taste of what they are searching for, the experience leaves them more determined to press on for whatever might satisfy them. They believe it is out there; they just have to find it. Sad isn't it to learn that these individuals lack the inner substance they need to identify what is real and what is a false reality? Until they find out what is on the "inside," they will not come to that wholeness and fullness they seek "outside." They need to come to a place of rest and reflection. They need to decide to do a different path, a different lifestyle.

If you find yourself on this roller coaster again, there is hope. There are answers for you. The question is, do you want to change???

Do you want to stop running "to"?

The "Around" Runners

Before we delve deeper into these personality types, let us look at the group that runs around. These persons are excellent at treating the symptoms and never dealing with the cause of a thing. They look for the shortest way, the fastest route, the least expensive, the band-aid approach, regardless of the downside or the potential repercussions their actions might cause. A great example of this would be one who suffers tremendous pain, swelling, and discomfort because of a seafood allergy. This allergy might cause gout or some other malady, but the individual will choose to take a pill prescribed by a physician, which often brings about other side effects, rather than adjust their diet to exclude the cause of the problem. This group refuses to deny the self. And they refuse to face the self with regard to discipline. Self is on the throne of the heart. Pleasing oneself, even at the expense of others or themselves, is the order of the day.

Our lives as a whole are filled with illusions. All the elements surrounding us from the day of our conception and birth, play a role in how we ultimately think and respond to the world around us. It's no wonder that one would have to renew the mind in order to have any chance of coming into the full knowledge of what makes a person who they are and why they "run" the way they do.

Think of running for a moment as an aphrodisiac. Something

inside of us reinforces that pattern of running. As fragmented individuals, complex, to say the least, our whole being hinges on what drives, motivates, or speaks to us inwardly. Our outer layer does not define who we really are and why we do what we do.

The fact that we run has nothing to do with notoriety or obscurity. It's not even about being rich or poor or anywhere in between. It has everything to do with who we are and how we interpret the world around us. From our interpretations and learned behavior, we create a pattern that consciously and very often unconsciously works for us until something happens to disturb the status quo. That something is often enlightenment or illumination. Until we come to a real knowledge in our mind and heart that "this behavior isn't doing or accomplishing what it needs to, we keep doing what we do." Until we can come to an honest evaluation of who we are and why we are, we can't begin an alternative course of action. This is a personal decision; it must come from the heart if you decide you want to change your behavior.

Years ago, I watched a movie starring Mary Tyler Moore (Fennigan, Begin Again.) It was about a man and woman who had found each other late in life, but one of them was more afraid than the other to take a chance on committing to this relationship and moving ahead together. The past had played such an important role as to why current choices were so difficult. Running from this type of involvement had been easy and accepted until now. There was something, in this case, someone, who was making it difficult to move ahead as usual. The man did not want to lose this woman, but he did not want the chore of beginning and investing all over again at this stage in life in a relationship that might not work out. But he had to make a choice. She too, had to make a choice. Was she going to settle for less than she wanted (so as not to be alone?) For the first time in many years, genuine feelings and a real zest for life were on the table. And the choice that had to be made was simply this—do I run, or do I begin again?

What's on the table for you today? What's tugging at your heartstrings? Do you keep running or stop here and now, evaluate…and then begin again? Do we make the decision to stop running around?

Examining the Belief System of the Runner

Until I felt the break, life's chains held me hostage. I had been living a runaround life. Think for a moment about a dog on an extended chain in a backyard. While he can move around in his particular space, pacing, running back and forth around its little doggie house or maybe a tree, his movement is hampered. It becomes obvious when the dog, by nature, wants to move outside of the chain link's length; a hard tug on the neck reminds the animal that while he can run about, there are limitations. Because of the chains, the best movement will be within that boundary that has been preset by the length of the chain.

Because of my conditioning as a child for years, I formed my own opinion about others, how they should think, how they should behave, etc. So, because of these thoughts, perhaps accurate to a small degree at times, I made decisions solely based on information that I believed to be true. At some point in life, we have all been guilty of this.

Whenever some incident would occur to challenge my belief system, I would simply put my personal spin on it or make some minor adjustments, but I would not see the root cause of the situation. You see, it had to be as I thought it to be because to be any different would mean that I was thinking wrong or hence, living a lie. An excellent example of this would be as follows:

A woman I once worked with was a talker. She couldn't allow silence to hover in a room for more than a few seconds, so she ultimately drove her co-workers to the brink of their endurance with the incessant chatter. As people would get up and walk out of the room or put up their hand and/ or pick up the phone to pretend they needed to make a call or even pick up a stack of work to move to another location to do their work, she told herself that they were being anti-social. After all, she was not the problem, so she just kept on talking. Her thoughts concerning herself were that she was a friendly person. She was taught to always be friendly in every situation. She was also taught that if a person remains quiet too long, they must be up to no good. This was pounded into her as a child. So as a child, she formed her assessment of how one would behave to ensure that everyone around her would know that she was a good person. Thus, she wanted her colleagues to know she was very good at this particular job. So, to give the right impression, she kept talking, and finally, one day, one of her co-workers just couldn't take it anymore! They blew up and railed all manner of what the talker felt to be cruel and devastating words. Then the woman broke down and cried as if she had had a nervous breakdown. Needless to say, this shocked the talking woman to silence, perhaps for the first real-time in her life. She was taken out of the office to a conference room, where the supervisor explained to her what had just happened. "Your co-worker just melted down from too much talking. You are a good worker, but you just talk too much. Perhaps this is not the place for you." How do you think the talker handled this situation? The talker still wanted to believe that the main problem belonged to others. Because to believe that her value system was wrong meant that she was wrong. So, this young woman chose to believe that she wasn't appreciated where she was so that she would leave, and that's exactly what she did. Unfortunately for her, this was not a wise choice that she would ultimately come to realize later in life.

You see, to believe what her supervisor told her, she had to accept that there was nothing wrong with silence. The idea that whenever it is too quiet in a room, something bad or evil is going on is already embedded in her belief system, put there by her parents. And because she did not want to be associated with bad or evil in any way, she made certain that any room she was in was not silent. Thus, she told herself that those around her must want to participate in evil or bad works; otherwise, they would help keep the chatter going.

A change could not occur for the chatterbox until her belief about silence changed. Because she was not ready to change her belief system, she continued this pattern that kept her locked in running around the problem. Are you running around an issue because it will require you to take a good hard look at your belief system?

Belief systems carry a lot of weight with who we are internally. They are placed there by many experiences and environmental factors. When this pattern of what we have come to believe as truth is reinforced in some way, it becomes a major part of our makeup. It's hard to crumble. It's very hard to find yourself standing on a foundation that's falling apart. Fear causes us to hold on tight. We tell ourselves that we have to do whatever we have to do to keep holding on to what we have been taught to believe is right. However, when this foundation crumbles and you find yourself standing in the ashes of your once safe place, then and only then will you consider making a change. This is a hard and hurtful place. But it is a necessary place if one is to take a good hard look at his/her belief system.

Because the belief system is so deeply rooted in one's soul, one does not always understand consciously why one does what they do. Rarely do people readily welcome intrusion in this aspect of their lives. So, the answer for them is to avoid it at all costs. Letting go is hard and in some cases, we make it harder on ourselves. Ultimately, if the runner is to stop running and face the challenge before him/her, they must wholly accept that they must allow something within them to die. On the outside, the horse is dead, but on the inside, the runner keeps beating it because accepting that it's time to let the belief system die is not acceptable to the conscious state of mind.

What are you holding on to from the vast number of people who have poured something into your life? Do you still believe in what you were taught at the foot of someone else, a principle that is causing you great challenges in your current life? I am reminded of a young man who told me that God and Satan are brothers. I couldn't believe my ears. I personally had never heard such a thing, and quite frankly, I couldn't even understand his position. So, I asked him where he ever got such an idea. He told me that his grandfather, who had raised him from a little tyke, told him that story many times, stressing that one was good and the other evil. And more importantly, he was taught that his grandfather always told the truth. No one in the family ever questioned his loyalty or his statements. There you have it; his grandfather did not LIE! A man, who had never told a single lie in his entire life, was at stake for this young man to believe differently. For him to accept that God and Satan were not brothers, he had to first accept that his grandfather was indeed a liar. His psyche was not able to deal with this truth, so he'd rather sound like an idiot or unlearned person than to risk letting go of a long-held belief that simply could not be true.

Facing the Real Enemies

We live. We grow. We change on the outside. But what happens on the inside of us? Many remain stagnant and unyielding. There are many reasons, but they can almost all be found in the following three categories: fear, doubt, and a lack of knowledge.

Most of us fear the unknown, so we avoid it as long as possible. We run from it. Many of us lack confidence in ourselves or others, so we also avoid situations that would make our confidence or lack thereof manifest itself. And because of this lack of knowledge, so many of us know so little about who we really are or about the world we find ourselves in that instead of standing still and finding out some answers, we just keep running around the real issues. We live life according to how it has been shaped by others instead of finding out how to come into our own. Self-evaluation becomes a necessary part of the equation if one wants a stable life. One must take the time to read and investigate what's important to us in our everyday life. We can't allow the "c'est la vie" approach to remain the order of the day. There comes a time when one must take control over what is coming into the eye and ear gates.

Often life is like a highway. There are major routes, roadways, and byways. There are side streets, boulevards, and alleys. There are lanes, circles, and cul-de-sacs, all of which you need signage in order to get from point A to point B and beyond. Without the aid of road routes, maps and posted signs, it would be nearly impossible to travel great distances.

We all face choices daily about which direction we should go and we face these choices at different stages in our lives. When we misread or misinterpret a sign, we can end up in a place where we didn't intend to be. So, our options are few but obvious. We stay where we are and make the best of it, to keep going in the wrong direction and hope for the best or turn around and go back to where we got off track and get on the right path, then proceed as originally planned.

Right now, you have a deep need in your life. That is why this book has found its way to you. You need to stop running long enough to evaluate where you are and where it is that you are trying to get to.

Let me share with you a story of someone who could have easily grown up and ran away from the challenges of life, but at a very young age, he faced it head-on.

Recently, I met a four-year-old little boy. His name is Jonathan, which means "my friend." I was so inspired by him that I had to write it down on paper to fully ascertain what I actually received from him.

He was sitting in a wheelchair. He had no use of his legs as they were strapped down to the wheel seat. He had limited use of one hand, and on the other hand, he did not move at all. Initially, I was unsure if he could speak, but because he followed me with his eyes, whenever I moved around the room, I asked his name from one of the other teachers as we moved from the classroom to the playground. Once we, the special needs students, and teachers were all situated outside, I walked over to Jonathan, said hello and called him by name. I did not expect a response, but I got a big surprise. Not only did he say hello back in a very strained voice, which seemed to take much effort to do, he proceeded to have a conversation with me.

He asked me what was hanging around my neck. It was my employee I.D. badge and my car keys, but again I made an assumption that he might not know that, so I tried to find some small word that he might understand but found none; I told him it was my badge for work with my picture on it.

He responded, "Oh, you work here?"

"Well, today I do," was my reply. I was substituting for his teacher.

"Where's Miss Ruddy?" he asked.

"I don't know," was my reply.

Then came the question, "Where do you live?" which I answered and then he added, "You have a lot of keys on your neck?"

"Well, yes, Jonathan, I suppose I do."

"Do you have a car?"

"Yes, I have a car." Then, he proceeded to ask me more questions:

"Is it here? Can I see it?"

"What color is it?"

"Will you take me for a ride in it?"

You get the picture!

There was one lucid question after another, and they were all in keeping with a logical flow of regular conversation. I was amazed. I remember asking one of the other teachers on duty, "Are you sure that he's only four years old?" She said he was just under three weeks from his 5th birthday, but as of this day, he was still only four years old. I could not believe that at first glance; I wasn't even sure that he could communicate at all. I learned a very important lesson; looks and assumptions can be very deceiving and misleading.

I recall leaving this experience very encouraged and very humbled. Many of us don't have nearly the obstacles that children like Jonathan have, yet we moan and groan and find all kinds of excuses to justify why we are not further along in our lot in life. It's always somebody else's fault that we didn't get the opportunity, or it's that unfortunate circumstance that just arrived at our door. We don't always take responsibility to learn what we should and put it to good use. So many of today's adults are slothful and careless with life's blessings; don't you be one of them?

You can do so much more and be so much more. Why not add up your assets, minimize your liabilities, and make up your mind to be better today than you were yesterday? Create a plan and follow it. Get a life coach if you have to. Visit http://www.powerup4success.net for additional information.

Jonathan knew very little about what life has to offer, yet he already lives like he isn't handicapped. He will go far. Because despite his physical limitations, he, at such a young age, has put no limitations on his mind. Biblically speaking, it is written that "a child shall lead." Let's follow Jonathan's example, take the limitations off, and live life to the fullest.

So, stop running from your own self-imposed limitations. Maybe you think you are too fat, or too short, or didn't get the right break or right opportunity. Perhaps you feel that you live on the wrong side of town and don't know the right people. Maybe others have told you that you won't amount to anything, or you take after a relative who lived a less-than-exemplary life. Maybe you are ashamed of where you work, or perhaps you don't work at all as you haven't been able to find a job. Whatever is holding you back or keeping you from moving in a direction that offers nothing positive to your life. Stop now! Sit down, rest awhile and re-evaluate some things. Add up the costs that you have already paid to be where you are, and if you are not satisfied with what you have, it's time to change course and head in a new direction.

The Unexpected

Change is inevitable. It's going to come into your life and challenge you, whether you want it to or not. Whether you benefit from it, grow from it, or remain stagnant, it's your choice, but you can't stop or alter its inception into your life! Change will challenge you. It will test you, pull you, prod you, and prick you. It will make you think; you must have lost or missed something important along the way.

Everything changes, like time, your mind, looks, ideas, emotions, situations, friends, finances, lifestyle, tastes, careers, etc. But there is one thing that never changes. It stays constant, and that is God Almighty.

You can welcome change like a bundle of joy, or you can find fault with it, or you can try to push it aside. You can try to run away from it or even hide from it. No matter what you choose to do or not to do, in order to welcome this parcel labeled change, it won't matter. It comes in any way!

When I left home on Saturday morning, October 29, 2005, I had visions of what my day would be like. I had even thought well into the evening what that would be like. I even had my next day and next week planned out. There was church, work, travel, real estate business, personal commitments, bills to pay, follow-up phone calls, etc. But something would so interrupt my Saturday that all those very important things would not get done, at least not by me anyway.

It simply amazes me how blindsided I was by this major event that was occurring in my life. I had been taught and even experienced in the past an intuition that "Holy unction," you know, the thing that lets you know something is about to happen. But, this time, nothing! This thing seemed to come out of nowhere.

Perhaps I'd come to a place of such "crowdedness" that I could no longer hear, see, or even sense danger. My focus was too narrow. I was feeling great! At least, I thought I was. Or perhaps, I was just in plain denial.

Denial is such a dangerous place because it won't let you see the dangers that await you in your future until you are one step past the safety zone! Gotcha!

Denial has such a strong pull on your present, which may seem to be blissful, pleasant, and uncomplicated. This creates a false sense of security. It's hard to believe that it's necessary to alter anything in your current situation, especially when all things seem to be good. Your perception is that everything will get better or, at best, remain the same. Wrong! Living in denial had caused many of God's creatures to be blindsided to approaching trouble.

But, oh, for the mercies of God, He still helps us and protects us despite our human frailties.

So, on this very exciting, perfect day, I am in a very good place. In a matter of a few hours, I will be conducting a very inspirational seminar, "Success Comes in Cans, not Can Not's!"

My morning was typical for the preparation of this seminar. In a matter of an hour, I had myself showered and dressed. Within the second hour, I printed off what materials I needed from the computer, packed the briefcase, and carried the bag. I made the phone calls necessary to verify lunch pickup and attendee pickups. I packed the car with ninety minutes to spare for my trip to pick up a friend and then reported to the hotel conference room for set up. Everything was going my way.

The seminar was a big success. Everyone who attended was open to the spiritual truths presented and the exchange from the group was awesome. God truly blessed us all to share and receive from one another. Then it was time to wrap up this session and plan for the next one.

Meanwhile, I needed to prepare for the two sermons I thought I would be preaching the next day. But, I had two more necessary tasks that had to be completed before I could turn my focus on the next day. First, I had to take my guest back home, and second, take a ride with my family to show them the new home God had made possible for me to own. Within two hours, my life would change. I would be standing at that great door called change, and I never saw it coming.

It was decided that I would ride with my son and his family instead of driving out to the new home in my own vehicle, allowing them to follow. Even though we didn't know it then, it was an excellent decision.

The first 30 minutes of the ride were jolly, lite conversations and reflections of the lessons learned from the earlier teaching. There were a few remarks concerning the next day's event when suddenly, I felt a hard pain in my right side. It was noticeably different from any regular ache or pain I had come accustomed to having. I tried hard to ignore it. I shifted my weight; I asked my son to move up his seat to give me a little more legroom. I even gave the sleeping baby I had been holding to her sister so that I could find a position that would assist in alleviating this pain.

It was now 45 minutes into the ride. My daughter-in-law, who was driving, stopped so that I could go to the bathroom, thinking that might help. Needless to say, it did not. By the time we got to that beautiful new home, I was in too much pain to enjoy the grand walk-through with them. They were on their own. Within minutes, I knew that I needed medical help. I spoke up, "I need to go to the hospital!" It was then noted that we were at least an hour away from home, and my response was, "We'll have to find a hospital out here; I don't think I can make it that far anyway. So, we found an H sign and followed it.

For the next 14 days, Brandywine Hospital would be my home. By the time we got to the emergency room, the pain was so great that I barely remember much more than a wheelchair being brought to me and my son putting his hand on my forehead to pray for me. I don't remember when or how I was examined, how I got out of my clothes into a hospital gown. I barely remember a woman's voice saying the words, "It's a stone." I don't remember my family leaving or even being taken to another room from the emergency room. I heard talking; it seemed to come from afar, "Her right kidney, the stone is too large to pass on its own." Then silence.

Then somewhere in this quiet place, I looked up at an all-white ceiling. There was a wheelchair next to my bed. There seemed to be nothing else in the room. I had this uncontrollable urge to urinate. I tried hard to hold it. I wondered if there was a buzzer; I needed to call for a nurse. I was barely able to move my hands at first. Then suddenly, I knew I wasn't going to be able to hold back. Gush! Again and again, the urine flowed. It seemed like it was not going to stop. I was soaked; the bed was soaked. Tears came into my eyes. I didn't understand what was happening to me. Then a face was over my bed; it was a nurse. I felt shame. I opened my mouth, "I'm sorry, I couldn't help myself, I tried not to, but it came anyway. But you don't have to do anything, you don't have to clean me up; I'll do it myself and if you bring me the sheets, I'll make the bed too; I'm so sorry," then the tears came like floodgates. I covered my face as I cried. And then I heard the gentlest voice saying to me, "I can't do that, honey, I can't let you lie here like this, let me help you."

I don't really remember how the other person got to the room or when. Everything began to fade in and out. I felt myself being shuffled from side to side, and I felt hands under me and around me. The wetness was going away; my gown wasn't wet anymore, then quiet again. I felt so helpless, so ashamed.

Then I heard voices again, "Her temperature it's going up again, it's 103. Call the doctor; we got to get her temperature down." I felt something on my arm tightening; a thermometer was in my mouth. Something was attached to my chest and sides. Something was in my nose. I was trying to move my head, my hands; I wanted to speak out, but nothing. Then it was quiet again.

I woke up as if from a dream. I looked around; I wasn't home. I was in a hospital room. A nurse came up to my bed and bent down over me. "I had to come," she said, "I was worried about you last night; you were a very sick lady on my watch; I'm glad we got that temperature to come down." She hugged me. I felt like she cared, and I didn't even know her name.

A little later in the morning, I would learn that this was the beginning of my third day in the hospital. A doctor, who had been assigned to me, came in to see me. He explained that my right kidney had been blocked by a huge stone, which brought on severe pain. However, after receiving my lab results, they discovered my blood count was too low to deal with the procedure to remove the stone. So, they put in a device called a stint, a temporary measure until they could raise my blood count, which was at seven. I needed a blood transfusion, which I had to sign for. He handed me the papers and further explained that after I was stabilized, they would then take care of the stone. Within twenty-four hours after the transfusion, my blood was drawn again to check its level, and it was as if I had never been transfused. Red flag! The doctor now knew something else was going on, and he immediately called in a hematologist and a GI specialist. They needed to know why I was losing blood internally. Other tests were ordered, one being the stress test. However, in order to take that test, my blood pressure had to be under control. It was then that the nurses were having trouble getting my blood pressure. Three tried but couldn't get it. The head nurse was called in, and he set the meter higher than 180. Then my blood pressure registered at 203 over 187. Wow! Much too high! In fact, it was at stroke level, and still, I was conscious and rejecting this reading. I told them that they should get another machine and take my pressure again because that reading couldn't possibly be right. I heard one nurse say to another one, "Call her doctor, stat." I thank God that they weren't listening to me at this point. I was in total denial concerning this issue. Next, I recall them bringing me two pills; one called Lopressor and the other Norvasc. They took my blood pressure every 10 minutes until it was back in the normal range. But because of this, I was unable to do the stress test by walking; they had to simulate it by giving me an injection. This caused me a great deal of pain and I failed the test. This led to them ordering a cardiac catheterization, which confirmed that there were no blockages to my heart and that my heart was fine, but there was way too much pressure in my pulmonary gland. Thus, a CAT scan was ordered. But just before the CAT scan, I was to undergo a colonoscopy. The night before this procedure, I had to drink a gallon of the most horrid water. In my mind, I was thinking, when will this all be over and I can just go home? It was day five now, and I had just been told that I would need another blood transfusion. And I would now be put on iron therapy because I was anemic.

The colonoscopy revealed two polyps in my colon and the endoscopy confirmed that a hiatal ulcer was still active. The polyps were removed and another medication, proto-nix, was added to the blood pressure medication and the iron. On Saturday morning, I requested to go home, promising that I would be very careful and follow the doctor's orders. I didn't even understand how sick I was. All I was trying to do was get away from those needles. Yes, I was trying to run away from this necessary interruption in my life. I was stuck so many times, and my arm and hands were so bruised. I was on a liquid diet, and I just felt like I was getting worse instead of better, so I wanted to just go home. Not long after the CAT scan, another doctor came in and behind her were two other hospital staff carrying an IV pole and two clear liquid-filled bags.

"Well, we can't send you home, and it looks like you will be with us for a while; we found a pulmonary embolism." She could tell by the look on my face that I had no idea what she was talking about.

"Have you ever heard of blood clots? Well, we just discovered that you have two of them on your right lung!"

Talk about change! It had just slapped me hard across the face.

I was stunned. I felt like this couldn't be happening. She kept talking about the treatment. I was now going to receive a blood thinner called heparin for the next several days. A Foley catheter was inserted in my bladder because they needed to measure my output. I couldn't hold back the fear in my eyes. I wanted someone there with me to hold my hand. To tell me that it was going to be all right. But my family had already been there for their visit that day and had returned back home, which was an hour's drive from this particular hospital. I felt so alone. By this time, I was with my third roommate; it would be ten altogether. She tried to comfort me, but I felt that I needed something, something that no human being alone would be able to give me.

My mind was spinning. Just like that, my whole life was out of control, and there was nothing I could do about it. All my hopes of being patched up and sent back out into the arena I knew so well were gone. This was serious. This time I wouldn't so easily be let off the hook. No more business as usual, a patch job and after a few days of rest, I would return to my old habits. If I had an ache, I took a pill. If I needed a little medical attention, I went to the doctor or the hospital, got a few days patch job at the most and I was back home again, living out my daily routines, doing what I believed to be important.

I was now in a place I had never been before, and this time I was going to have to deal with my life, my decisions, and my health issues. This time I wasn't going to be able to push aside what was happening to me. I wasn't going to be able to deny the invasion that was attacking my body. I wasn't going to deem something or someone else more important. I couldn't run away from things. This time, it was indeed just me and God, and He had my attention. No more running away and no more running around!

Here I am lying on my back in a hospital bed for eight days now, hooked up to IV, heart monitor, blood pressure pump, a catheter in my bladder, a stint in my urethra, oxygen tubes in my nose, blood being drawn from my veins every twelve to twenty-four hours, nurses bringing me five to seven pills every four to six hours. I was sore, bruised, black and blue. My emotional agony rivaled my physical pain. I tried hard not to ask the question, why? I was determined to hold on to the one name that would make all the difference, Jesus. I was actually afraid to think outside of that parameter. Jesus, help me, was all I would allow myself to think about; it would be all I would allow myself to say out loud when I looked around at my condition.

I went back in my mind trying to at least figure out what signs I had missed that caused me to be in this place.

Was it two years ago when I was hospitalized for anemia and internal bleeding? I received three blood transfusions from that brief hospital stay of four days. Did I not properly follow up with my outpatient care? Had I taken the fact that I was anemic too lightly? After all, I had heard this term all my life. And yet Momma, who was anemic and Daddy, who was anemic, lived to be 67 and 56 years old. Momma died of diabetes, and Daddy from a heart attack. Had anemia played any role in those deaths?

Or did this episode begin three years ago, when I went on a cruise ship for the first time? I collapsed on the deck of the ship with a blood pressure reading of 181 over 106. I chalked it up to fear of being on a ship in the middle of the ocean. I always ran away from anything, any truth that I didn't want to believe. Even though I was monitored very carefully for the balance of the cruise, did I take it too lightly that I had a blood pressure problem when I returned home and not try too hard to find medication to control it? You see, I didn't like the doctors telling me that I would be on medication for the rest of my life for this malady, so I chose to believe that I had no blood pressure problem, even though it was also a condition that ran in my family. By my sheer will, I was just going to eat right, exercise, praise God for my good health and ignore anything that said otherwise. After all, I felt like I wasn't going to stick with this trial-and-error method of finding the right blood medication for me just to have to take it all my life. I didn't like taking pills except to get rid of the problem and then move on.

I thought about work; how, for the last 10 to 12 years, it had been a high priority. After all, I had to be self-sufficient. A divorced woman in her late 40s then and unwilling to participate in illicit love affairs to get help from men, made me a prime candidate for workaholism. I didn't have time to be sick. I needed to keep going until one day, my change would come. However, the change I had in mind was not sickness.

And, oh yes, there was the ministry. I can't forget about the work that God called me to do. This teaching ministry required so much time that, in actuality, I was working two full-time jobs without even realizing it. Because my life was so full of doing, giving, helping, and working, I rarely spent the necessary time with God in prayer. Oh, I said the two-to-five-minute prayer daily. I often quoted the Lord's Prayer. I occasionally went down on my knees. From time to time, I participated in corporate prayer. I was always in contact with God, at least, I thought I was. You see, what I missed was that my life was so hurried and so full of one activity to another that I lost focus on what was important. I lost my ability to hear that small, still voice and became a driven person.

Then too, there were so many people in my life, and I tried to stay connected to them all. Now I lay here in this hospital bed, searching for answers. My mind is racing, I can't sleep. Here comes the nurse now with a shot. Starting on day ten, I would receive a shot in my stomach every 12 hours. It burned like fire. "Jesus, help me!"

Even though I felt fear swelling up inside of me, I wouldn't dare let it come from my lips. I had to believe God. I desperately needed to hold onto His Word, that he would never leave or forsake me. I needed to believe that he was right there with me, knowing and feeling and understanding everything I was going through. I was clinging to those precious truths that I had been taught, truths that I also taught others. I reminded myself that Jesus had taken stripes on His own flesh for my healing, that He had been wounded for my transgressions. I reminded myself that, above all, He wanted me to prosper and be healthy; His Word has taught me that if I abide in Him and He abides in me, I could ask for what I will, and it would be done unto me. I recalled the scripture, which it stated that the fervent prayer of the righteous availed much.

I knew in my heart that many people were praying for me and I held on to the belief that God was hearing those prayers because they were coming from His children, who were righteous because of their relationship with Jesus Christ.

I know it gets hard to keep on believing when everything around you just keeps falling down. But I had to go through with this. There were some lessons I had to learn. I was going through it for a reason, even though it was not quite clear to me.

My son and daughter-in-law brought their pastor to have prayer and Holy Communion with me. My daughter and son-in-law brought me a T-Shirt to remind me that Christ was in the midst of this very chaotic situation. I received the same get-well balloon from two friends with Psalm 91:11 printed on it. "He shall give his angels charge over thee…"

I received several visits from friends and other pastors, phone calls and emails from extended family and friends. And even though I couldn't deal with the phones or emails for a time, they left me encouraging words that I so needed to hear them. God is truly amazing. As hard as it was, I was keeping still. No running away from this.

As day eleven approached, a sister in Christ helped me to locate the word of God that was attaching itself to my spirit. That word was Psalms 118:17, "I shall not die, but live and declare the works of the Lord." I could not sleep many nights, so I watched Trinity Broadcasting Network, and every message I heard seemed to be especially for me. Even though I was weak in my body now, I felt strong in my spirit. I held on tight to the belief that I was going to go home soon. On the 12th day, I was told that my Pro Time level was too low to be discharged. It was only 1.6 and it had to be at least 2.0. By Friday, two days later, it was 2.3. I cried. There was one little vein that they were able to find on me, a vein that they were never able until now to draw blood from, and it was the only one that was working. It gave them what they needed and I was allowed to go home. I was cautioned that I was not yet stable and had to return to the hospital on Monday. I agreed. I just wanted to go home.

But alas, going home on that Friday afternoon was not what I thought it would be. I was very weak, and I was bleeding too much. When I returned to the hospital on Monday, they found that my Pro Time levels were too high, 4.7. At max, they could only be 3.0. I had to be readmitted to the hospital for another 4 days. A song came to my mind that the Lord had given me to write many years ago, "My Loving Lord Knows Best!" And it was the third verse in particular:

And when the storms began to roll, as I surely know they will, I'll remember that watchful night; my Lord said, peace be still, I'll never leave you or forsake you; I'll help you climb that hill, for its only but a test, yes it's only but a test, for my loving, loving Lord, He knows what's best.

For truly, I was being tested and carried in a way as never before. These untreaded waters held the formula for success, failure, faith, fear, trust, or unbelief. I had come too far now to fall to failure, fear, or unbelief. And then I was reminded of another song that God had given me many years ago:

"I'm gonna trust my Jesus, I'm gonna trust His Word, I'm gonna trust my Jesus, I'm gonna trust my Lord.

He told me in His Word that he would never leave me.

Never forsake me and always would forgive me.

So, I'm gonna trust my Jesus, I'm gonna trust His Word.

If you look around you, Satan is everywhere, filling lives with trouble, strife, and despair.

But if I follow Jesus, Satan can't hold me down,

He can't steal God's glory and I will wear my crown.

Hallelujah, I'm gonna trust my Jesus; I'm gonna trust His Word."

So, upon being readmitted, I was confident that God was in control. Those doctors would be able to stop the internal bleeding. They would be able to administer the right antibiotics to kill the infection attempting to invade my bladder. They would be able to regulate the medicines to safe therapeutic levels. And, whatever else remained to be done to bring about stabilization would happen. I knew this. I now understood they could accomplish this because all control concerning me was not with them. It was with God. He had been guiding them all along to dis- cover all the things that had gone wrong with my body. God was in complete control. Everything that concerned me concerned him. He had brought me this far on broken pieces. He had allowed me to get up from that place of sickness and to remain here in the land of the living, on this side of the Jordan. God had an entirely different life planned for me and no devil in hell was going to interfere with His plans. I had only to believe in Him.

I know in my heart that I could not have survived this ordeal had it not been for the Lord on my side. I thank Him that in the midst of my doubts, my uncooperativeness, and my human frailties, He didn't give up on me. I praise Him and I know that my life will never be the same as it was before.

Today, one day before the celebrated holiday, Thanksgiving, I sat in the living room of a brand-new home. God made this possible. Looking out over the quiet neighborhood, I felt so blessed to be alive. I am now looking forward to God's new direction for my life. I no longer desire to live a life that I think is pleasing to God; I want to live the life that is pleasing to God. He has given me so many gifts that I have never used or have underutilized because I felt inferior to others and their talents.

So going forward, I know that as long as I follow His lead and stay connected to Him, I will be all right, always To God be the Glory, and I declare the works of the Lord. I am truly thankful! Through this, I am learning to lean on Him, not on what I think. I see life now through different eyes. Except for the Grace of God, none of us would have a chance at eternal life or living in victory down here on earth.

I understood before that sickness is not always unto death, but now I know along with that truth that sickness has a divine purpose. God is faithful in his purpose. He will complete the work that he begins. Whatever it takes to get our attention, He will allow. I thank God that he got mine. One of the five attending physicians said it best when he summed up my situation on the eighteenth day of my hospital stay after signing my discharge papers for the second time.

"I'm glad we could help any one of the four ailments you suffered while here was enough by itself to take you out; you had all four at the same time and you are still here!"

How does that grab you? Only to God be the glory!

WHAT MATTERS MOST IS HOW YOU SEE YOURSELF

The Danger of Building Walls

Now, let me address the many of us and perhaps many of our population, who have just run away from very disappointing circumstances of some kind. Perhaps it was a loved one or a very close friend, someone who hurt you or disappointed you deeply. Your emotions have been all over the place. You've tried not to feel the pain. You've told yourself; it doesn't matter on the grand scale of things. You have tried to lay it aside, but it follows you. In some cases, you can't even sleep. So, you finally go to that place where you decide that the very best solution is just to cut yourself off from this whole situation, including the person. You shut down, vowing never to let this type of pain or disappointment enter again. You make your decision to go away and stay away final! You don't call or visit, and you don't receive any calls or visits should they happen to come in your direction. You don't write, email, or text. In fact, you delete any contact info from all your lists. There will be no more investment of time from you at all. But…

In the grand ole scheme of things, all you have done is build a wall that will crumble one day when you least expect it. Why? Because you haven't dealt with the pain or the disappointment. You have also failed to realize that whatever this situation was, it happened in your life because there was a necessary change that needed to take place in your very own character development. You can't come forth and be all that you were created to be without pruning. The very fact that pain and disappointment stopped you from facing life head-on should tell you something. You are not ready to deal with any opposition greater than what you have just encountered. You see the world as full of enemies that will surely come against you that have no interest in seeing you succeed. While close friends and loved ones can and will sometimes hurt us, they can also be forgiven and can find their way back to us. But in order for that to happen, we must leave the door open. And to do that, we must find a way to face the hurt, deal with it, and move on. Running away from it is not the answer.

One of the saddest things about running away from responsibility and growing up is that it drastically impacts your reputation. Don't you know this fact? Your name arrives at a destination before you do. When people hear your name, it creates an image in their minds and an opinion in their souls.

I remember an elderly relative of mine who used to say to me as a child; your word is your bond. I didn't understand it then, but he was teaching me that whatever I said, I should do it because I would become known by my actions as they lined up with what I said. The world is full of people who will say one thing and then do another. And they see nothing wrong with their behavior. They also get upset when they are not believed or taken seriously when something they deem to be important is not treated the same way by those around them. So, what do they do? Run! Yes, run from the very fact that they created a negative reputation and put the blame on somebody else. Facing truths about yourself is hard, especially if you have become accustomed to lying to yourself.

Have you lied to yourself lately? Are you lying to yourself about anything now?

Many of life's lessons are crammed inside of inspirational quotes. Now is a good time to reflect on some of them.

Corrie Ten Boom wrote: "The first step on the way to victory is to recognize the enemy."

Most of us are running from, to, around, or away from responsibility or pain of some kind. This quote reminds us that we all have a common enemy that will stop at nothing to see that we fail. This common enemy presents itself in many forms:

This Enemy shows up in the following places:

1. A loved one…those closest to you have your heart, so what they think is important to you…

2. A missed opportunity…when you learn of a specific event or celebration that you so wanted to be a part of, but for some reason, it escaped your radar until that moment had passed…

3. A misunderstanding…not being in agreement with some aspect of your life or person who is important in some way can be painfully stressful and upsetting, but to learn that no harm was intended after the damage has been done, does cause distrust to some extent going forward…

4. A not so successful day at school or work… every day does not turn out the way we expect and sometimes we are not in a place mentally or emotionally to deal with it…

5. A desire that goes continually unfulfilled…there are times when that deep yearning just wants to be heard, wants to be fed, but life is still getting in the way…

6. A lack of being appreciated…so many times, we find ourselves in a place of feeling like no one cares how often or how much we put out. No one seems to care that we have needs as well, and whose taking care of them while we so tirelessly take care of others?…

7. A lack of support…do you have a support system? If not, you owe it to yourself to put one into place.

8. Being taken for granted…no one likes to be taken for granted. We all have an inherent need to be appreciated. I read in a book somewhere several years ago that we need to spend time with people who celebrate us, not just tolerate us.

9. Believing in a lie…lies are told to us from time to time and we find ourselves believing them because we want to; it's time to face the truth and leave the lies on the shelf. We especially need to stop lying to ourselves.

Breaking a promise or commitment Burning the wrong bridges Complaining instead of making efforts to correct. Chasing after foolishness.

This list could go on and on. The enemy of our souls can and does show up in all these situations to help us make up our minds to give up, give in and just avoid these issues altogether, to treat them as nothing and just move on. However, another wise sage would say to us at this point that "the wise person will own his/her decision to stand fast (face these challenges) while the ignorant will be swayed by public opinion"…or their own self-defeating emotions.

Next in this line-up is, "Adversity is a refining pot that opens up a door to opportunity."

No one likes adversity, but it is necessary because, as human beings, we are creatures of habit and comfort. As long as we are comfortable in a thing, we won't budge. It takes something that makes us uncomfortable to get us to move or stir or to even look at alternatives. If you are trying to move forward in your life in any way, it won't happen if you don't put an effort behind it. Not efforts that require you to avoid the uncomfortable place by running away, but efforts that will cause you to create a new plan of action and then follow through.

It's important to know that a true soldier does not admit or accept defeat before he faces the battle. He will take all he has and all he is and all he knows and all he believes to be true and courageously go into battle and fight for the outcome he desires. And if he dies in battle, so be it; he dies fighting for what he believes in and what his life stood for. Are you getting to a place where you are willing to stop running and start fighting?

Early in the 1920's Max Ehrmann wrote a very relevant and powerful piece of prose that lets all of us as humans know that, without a doubt, we have a right to be here. Our purpose is amid the path we must travel. We get to where we are to go, not by running away from those things we come into contact within this world but by realizing and accepting that we have a place and choices to make regarding that time, a place that we occupy. We have a responsibility to ourselves and it is about time that we recognize it.

One of His Own

Several weeks ago, as I pondered for something different to deliver as a sermon on Easter Sunday, I became still and started reflecting on how often we follow tradition on certain matters and how we continue to move in the same direction. We may dress up the words or introduce a new angle, but still, we follow the same pattern of delivery. But this time, I wanted to run with something different, so it required something different from me. I had to hush the voices and the known approaches to a very familiar event. As I sat quietly and listened to my inner thoughts, one simple phrase entered: "One of his own."

I allowed my mind to think of this single thought until it carried me to a question.

The question was, "Are you one of his?"

I quickly responded, "One of whose?"

Before long, I was having an internal conversation with myself and I felt excitement swell from the inside of me. I jotted down the few words, as I did not want to forget them and then I continued to be still. Then Moses, from the Bible, popped into my mind. I knew his story like I knew the back of my hand, but never had I thought about him as one of God's own, chosen to be the deliverer of the Israelites.

These people had been in bondage for hundreds of years, and the Pharaoh was a cruel taskmaster. If deliverance was ever going to come, it had to be a Godly intervention and a Godly intervention it was. God took one of his own people out of his nation and caused it to be so that he would grow up in the Egyptian nation with an Egyptian, learning the ways and laws of the Pharaoh, growing up in his palace, eating from his table and yet, would eventually be used for the purpose of facing the Egyptian Hierarchy to set a nation free. It had to be an inside job and it had to be from one of God's choosing. Moses ran from his fate, but he still had to return to do the job he was called to do. There were many runners in the Bible. Jonah tried to run away from Nineveh, choosing another direction, but in the end, he had to stop running, repent and do what he was called to do. David tried to run from his wrongdoings when he took Bathsheba and then had her husband killed in battle. But still, God sent Nathan to him to expose him for who he was and again, David had to stop running from the truth. There were so many of our Bible heroes who tried to run away from the call on their life, but they somehow had to come to a place of understanding that is running only delayed the inevitable.

How about you? Have you taken into consideration that running away does not solve problems altogether?

Many years ago, Kenny Rogers sang a song, "The Gambler," about knowing when to make the right decisions.

Running to, from, or for something needs to be weighed in the light of the circumstances and then acted upon accordingly. But it should not, by no means, be a way of life. To stop running means you have to face up to some reality. Cowards don't like to do this. They find it easier to run, run, run. But you know what? One day the legs will get tired, the mind will get tired, and the heart will grow weary; what then? Will you check out of life altogether? Many folks have tried it, and some have succeeded, but the shame of that is it is such a waste of life. Living does not have to be a chore; it can be a joy. It is a journey where you do not have to travel alone or in a hurry.

The Gift of Waiting

Waiting…This is one word that runners don't like to hear. These runners are anxious. They seem to have a need to move constantly, consistently. So when asked or told that they need to slow down to a halt or that they need to wait or rest, it seems to be out of the equation.

To wait also means to stop moving forward inwardly as well as outwardly. One must consider giving the mind time to relax and move away from the constant activity imposed on it.

Waiting can cause one to come face to face with the real challenge, the real problem, and the real solution.

Facing oneself is not always easy. Self usually has an inflated ego or a misconception of what truth really looks like and sounds like.

No one wants to hear that he or she is incapable of making the right decisions for themselves, even though it may be true on some level. Not many want to hear that they need to face up to the discord that they, themselves, have brought into the lives of themselves and others.

So, what, then, is the solution? The act of waiting alone can't possibly turn things around, or can it?

When waiting or slowing down, one's desire or need to run causes a new experience to surface. One has time to think, feel, and look within to find a hidden strength. Many people believe in God but just don't know how to reach for him or how to feel his presence in their lives. Many want to know if God is real and if He will move in their life. Perhaps this is what you are thinking right now. If there is a God, why doesn't he move? Why doesn't He allow me to know that He is here with me and that He, indeed, is real? God has three distinct personalities. While He is indeed One, He also represents Himself in the flesh, just like yours and mine and He represents Himself in Spirit inside of you and I. He can be assessed but only by faith. Yes, there is that word, faith.

You have probably heard it before, but it bears repeating that faith is what it takes to move the hand of God upon your life.

Watch God Move

How many of us would like to see the hand of God move? His hand moved when:

The 10 commandments were written on the tablets of stone before given to Moses.

1. Luke 26:36—When He reclaimed the Spirit of Jesus, who had commanded it to go back to God.
2. In Your life and mine when God gave His only begotten Son to whosoever will…

God will continue moving in our lives if we will just grab hold of His truth and operate in it. Many of us in this room right now know a lot about God's truth. We can recite many passages of scripture in this Bible. But often, we don't operate in these truths; we don't act on them. Oh yes, we say them out loud, and we even quote them to one another when the moment calls for it, but when left to our own devices and our own thoughts and duties, some find themselves making excuses not to move on or act on God's words.

Excuses like:

1. I am not good enough
2. I don't deserve this
3. I am too tired
4. I don't have time today
5. I have something more important on my plate right now
6. I can't do everything, let somebody else do this
7. This is too hard
8. It's more effort than I want to put out
9. My body hurts
10. I have a headache
11. I am not feeling all that well
12. I don't have any help; I can't do it alone
13. I don't have the money it would take, so that I won't do anything
14. I just can't put myself out there; people should do for themselves

We don't want to tell ourselves the truth; it's just too ugly. So the devil helps us make it sound good, so we can stay right where we are:

1. Just let them know that if your circumstances were different, you would do more and sound sincere

2. Just ask them to pray that you will get there because right now, it's too hard for you to get to that place from where you are coming from.

3. Everyone gets tired; you are no different. After all, you have a lot on your plate that others don't even know about, and you work very hard at what you do get involved in; never mind that its other people's business or someone else's responsibility that has you are so tired, never mind that it's those pleasurable things that you prefer to put ahead of God's time, that's not the issue, the issue is I'm tired so until I rest, I just can't do anything more…

4. My priority is my priority; it's nobody's business. And you know what? You are correct. However, there is one fallacy in that statement, while it is nobody's business in the human sense, it is God's business. His business is paramount to yours and mine. We name the name of His dear Son, so the priority is no longer what we want but what He wants and we still like our lives are all about us and all about what we want. We live our lives to please ourselves and those whom we love in the flesh. And then tell God that He has to take a back seat.

5. What can be more important than God? But we treat Him as

the least important in our lives. We don't respect God's Time, Place, or His Guidance. We are bent on doing it our way. When was the last time you said Not my will, but Thine be done, and meant it?

6. We spend too much time waiting on someone else to do something to make our job easier for us. When they don't do what we think they should and the job is not done, we want to claim that it's not all our fault because somebody else didn't do what they were supposed to, so you were just waiting. Waiting can be dangerous and can have disastrous results.

7. Anything can look like it's too hard to accomplish as long as you just stare at it.

8. Some of us are just plain lazy, but we don't want to admit it. We'll admit to all kinds of ailments and limitations, but laziness, oh no, that's just not true. Because to admit to laziness, we would have to say the truth, and that is, I just don't want to do it. I want to do what I want to do that brings me pleasure and this is just work and sacrifice.

9. The devil loves it when you tell God's servants that you're not well, after all, no one expects you to do anything when you're sick. In fact, they will tell you to stay home, lie down, or see a doctor. They will tell you to do nothing, which is exactly what you want to hear so that YOUR conscience is clear but guess what. It isn't clear because, after a little while, those sick lies

will make your body sick.

10. Many times, when we walk with God, we will find ourselves walking alone. Everyone you know and everyone you might want to walk with you will not walk with you. Suppose you were standing at heaven's gate and the Lord opened it and told you to come on inside to your eternal reward but standing beside you was an earthly loved one who had not done what they needed to do to come on in; so, this is the parting moment; the invitation to come on in was not extended to them.; only to you. The clock is ticking and you have 5 seconds to go inside the gate, or it will close forever; what would you do? Many people who have gods other than God would hesitate for six seconds.

11. Money, oh, how the devil uses money against us and the kingdom and we have allowed this to happen so many times. When will we wake up to the fact that the Earth is the Lord's and the fullness thereof? When will we accept that God's word is true, that the righteous will not be forsaken nor His seed begging bread, when will we accept that God wants us to prosper and be in good health, that He has given us the power to get wealth and that no good thing will He withhold from us if we walk upright before Him? That if we pay our tithes and offerings, He not only will rebuke the devour for our sakes, but He will open the windows of heaven and pour us out a

blessing that we will not have room enough to contain. That our meal barrow will not end; we will be fed even in times of famine. That our needs will be met, He will not forsake us. But we just keep holding back on God and holding on to our seed that should be planted. OH, some do plant, but they don't plant where God tells them to and then they expect God to give them a harvest when they let the devil take their money.

12. People who don't know God will only see God through his people; what example are you showing?

Okay, so you haven't made a commitment of any kind to be referred to as one of God's own people. But you were created in your mother's womb by Him. I know that there is a popular belief that man got here through some off participle of a big bang theory or evolved from the ape species. But logically, those theories just don't hold up under real scrutiny. Like species can only produce after its own kind. Whatever is planted is what will grow. You can't plant an apple tree and get a walnut tree. You can't mate two baboons and get an elephant. All life as we know it had a beginning and it began with creation…God's creation. Just read Chapter One of the Old Testament in the Bible with an open mind and see life unfold from vegetation to mankind.

Problems Don't Just Go Away

Everyone, at some time or another, has experienced at least one problem. Even children encounter them. Some of us fret and fume, and some of us just cry and complain. Still, there are some of us who just try to run as far away from it as possible. But life has taught me some interesting things about problems.

1. They have endurance. They stand the test of time; they will not just dissolve.

2. They have X-ray vision. You can try to escape them, hide from them, retreat to any place you would like to, but still, they find you.

3. They have tenacity. Problems just never seem to get tired of sitting on your doorstep. They can outlast the toughest of individuals.

4. They have a built-in radar. Just when you think you have escaped their grasp, bam! They pop up just like that.

5. They are selfish. Problems want all of your time.

6. They are companion oriented. They want you all to themselves. They enjoy your company, morning, noon, and night, every single day. They are content to live with you all the days of your life.

7. They are cowards. Yes, problems are cowards, but you won't know that as long as you don't stand up to them. Leaving them in control will surely keep you in a cowardly mode, but the moment you take a stand, the moment you stop running from them, is the same moment that you discover that your problem is really not a match for

you.

Let's take a closer look at endurance. In the Bible, Book of Job, we find the godly servant, Job. He endured his problems to the very end, even though it looked like he was going to lose his life to them. From him, we learn that as long as we don't give up and hold on to that inner strength and belief, we can outlast any problem, even multiple problems. God created us and he knows exactly how much we can bear. When Job had been through the fire long enough, God stepped in and delivered his servant. He will do the same for you if you will just stop running.

Next, let's look at X-ray vision in the person of Nathan in the Book of Samuel 2. David was so sure that his sin was hidden from everyone, but God had revealed it to Nathan and Nathan confronted David. All of David's efforts to hide his sin had not worked. He was still found out and confronted. What might you be trying to hide from public scrutiny? If you don't deal with it, it will come back to bite you. Stop running from it and face it. Even if it means you have to go to others and ask for forgiveness, you will be amazed at the weight that will come off your shoulders.

Now for tenacity, the widow woman found in the book of Luke is a perfect example. She continually kept going before an unjust judge to get justice for her situation. They did not regard man nor God, but this widow was wearing him down. It got so bad that he just gave her what she wanted just to make her go away. Any problem you encounter will not just go away. It must be dealt with once and for all. When the judge dealt with this woman, she went away. Wouldn't you like to see that happen with the problems in your life? Then stop running from them and deal with them. If you just stop, be still, and look for it, there is a solution.

Now for the radar, Nehemiah would be a good subject for this aspect. Even though he had left the king for whom he worked for with permission, three intruders still sought him out, found him on the wall rebuilding, and still did all they could to try and stop his progress. I encourage you to map out your course and stick to it no matter what tries to stop you. Getting the job done despite anything will defeat your problem.

King Saul is an excellent example of how selfish our problems are. In 1 Samuel 18, we find King Saul consumed with the problems of his day. He consistently looked for the easy way out. He didn't want to face them head-on with the instruction that was God-given; he just wanted to do things his way and wanted them to work. Our human ways are no match for situations that must be fought spiritually. King Saul found this out much too late and he lost his kingdom and his life because of it.

And, as for companion oriented, here we will look at Samson in the book of Judges. He just had to go outside of his tribe to find strange women. These encounters caused him nothing but problems and more problems until finally, he no longer had the wisdom to fight against them and he succumbed to them. Not only did he lose his sight and life, but he temporarily lost his strength. He regained it long enough to complete his purpose on the earth. Sadly, he never had to have gone down this path, but he did. Many people today take a path that ensures that they will run into problems. Take a good look at your direction. Are you embarking on a path that will surely lead to unnecessary problems? If so, you might want to rethink your direction.

Facing The Giant—7 Days

Use this section of the book as a journal. It is now time for you to face the reasons why you run. Be honest with yourself. If you do not want to write your responses down inside this book, get a separate tablet and do so. But you must take the time to go through this experience. It's time to take a good look at where you are and where you want to go…

Rule #1: Don't move forward to the end of this segment until you have written down your responses.

Rule #2: Be painfully honest with your responses; remember, you don't have to share them with anyone else if you don't want to.

Rule #3: Use what you learn and now consciously realize to change your behavior, therefore, making a change in your life.

DAY 1. Take the first 15 minutes of this day and go to a quiet room, your back deck, or sit on a porch or even a bench in a park…you decide. In this book below, write down everything that you see in these 15 minutes. When the time is up, look over your list a few times. Then sit the book down for at least 4 hours. Don't move ahead.

When you come back, re-read what you have written down:

_____

_____

_____

Now that you have done this exercise answer the following questions:

In your observation, did you write down any "colors?" Did you write down any "shapes?"

Did you write down any descriptive words, such as "hard" surface or "soft" pillow?

The purpose of this exercise was to help you get in touch with what is really in your site path and how much of what you really take in from your environment. It is important to see the "little details" when you are about to tackle a challenge that has been a problem for you.

DAY 2. Today we want to write down the challenge you face in more detail.

Fill in the blanks:

I run (around, from or to) describe the situation, i.e., I run from sitting in a quiet room when people are present...

Now your turn:

Now answer this question:

_____

_____

_____

_____

_____

_____

_____

Why do I do this:

I run because

I don't

_____

_____

_____

_____

_____

_____

I want

_____

_____

_____

_____

_____

_____

I feel

_____

_____

_____

_____

_____

I have

_____

_____

_____

_____

_____

_____

_____

I can't

_____

_____

_____

_____

_____

_____

PUT THIS BOOK AWAY NOW UNTIL TOMORROW.

DAY 3. Re-read everything you wrote down yesterday and then pray about it. Do not take this lightly. It is necessary for you to be in touch with yourself. After all, you are discovering why you have been doing what you have done for so long.

DAY 4. Select one item that you want to tackle, just one. Then get yourself an accountability partner. This person must be someone who is not a yes person but someone whom you have a great deal of respect and will trust they will say to you. You want them to tell you the truth, and you want to receive the truth. You will want them to keep you on track until you get through this process. It may make you sad but be encouraged; the best is yet to be.

DAY 5. Write down what you need the outcome to be as you face up to your challenges. In other words, what is the payoff that you would like for yourself?

_____

_____

_____

_____

_____

_____

DAY 6. Repeat this process with the next item on your list.

DAY 7. Rest. Yes, rest and think about this past week. What was good about it? What would you like to continue? What would you not want to repeat?

Have you discovered that you are worth more than you give yourself credit for?

God made only ONE like you in this whole world and it was not and is not His intention to see you go through this life running away from those things that He sent you here to correct. Yes, we all have a purpose and you must get through some things in order to discover and complete your work here. After all, you have a part in leaving this place better than you found it.

Remember David, he faced the giant Goliath, and he won, but not on his own; he had God on his side. God is on your side, too, if you allow Him to be. He created you for greatness; now, face the challenge and change some things.

Putting It All Together

Confidence is a major key in helping one to stop running unnecessarily.

1. Think about someone who is confident. Observe how they act, talk, and walk. Talk with them, ask them questions, learn from him or her. If you care to, model their mannerisms and behavior. It works for them; you are free to try whatever aspect that you admire to see if it will work for you. Remember that you also have a personality, so you want to keep who you are while developing the attributes that you admire in someone else.

2. Smile a lot more. That doesn't mean putting a silly grin on your face! But smile when you walk down the street when you meet people and greet someone, look them in the face and smile. Smiles are contagious, they will come back to you.

3. Learn from the past; don't beat yourself up about it. It's gone; it's never coming back. Instead, learn from it for next time. Remember the old adage; "Don't cry over spilled milk!" Just clean up the spill and start the "pour" again, but this time, avoid what caused the spill in the first place.

4. Buy yourself some new clothes, get your hair done, and treat yourself to something new. It will make you feel better and will give your ego a boost. If you can't afford a new outfit, try the second time around shops. Often you can find good bargains there.

5. How prepared are you for new situations entering into your life? Is your preparedness enough to meet any challenge that may come up? Are you prepared for that next meeting, that next presentation, that next job interview, and even for when you meet someone for the first time? If not, get to it. Do your homework.

6. Perform in your strengths. Know what you are good at and expose yourself to these opportunities at every opportunity because you're good at it, you'll enjoy it and it will help you increase your confidence level.

7. Improve your weaknesses. Know and appreciate what these are and put a plan in place to improve them over time. Meanwhile, seek out friendships from colleagues who are strong in the areas that you are not. Do not fail to invest in yourself and your goals. Nothing in this world is absolutely free!

8. Learn how to say no to people who vex your spirit or just waste your time. Don't be afraid; you've got nothing to be afraid of. Just watch the reaction on their face after you've said it the first time and there will be no going back. Say yes to what you're passionate about and pursue it.

9. Be positive. Look on the "can do" side of things rather than the "can't do." You've accomplished lots in your life, and you will accomplish lots more in the future. After all, everyone has at least one gift/ talent. Use your gift to be a blessing to others as well as yourself. Remember that success comes in "cans," not in "I cant's!"

10. Be in charge of your thoughts at all times. What is a thought? It's just a question you've asked yourself and the thought is your answer. If you're thinking negative thoughts, you're probably asking a negative question. Change the questions to be more positive. For example, instead of asking yourself, "Why do I feel like giving up?" turn it around and instead ask yourself, "What can I do to keep going?"

11. Whenever you feel a negative thought coming, stop, think, and ask yourself, is this really important in the grand scheme of things? A lot of the time, it isn't. Many people seem to, in their lifetime, major in minor things! Don't you be one of those people. Subscribe today to the following blog: http://www.wisdomisthekey.wordpress.com.

12. Do you let the words of others affect you to the point of stopping you from pursuing your dreams? Try not to mind too much about what they think of you, especially if it is not in keeping with your character. Remember that no one can make you feel inferior without your consent. It's not what they say to you that's the problem, it's what you say to yourself after they have stopped talking that's the problem. Don't let others change the way you think about yourself. It's only their opinion.

13. List the words that you use on a consistent basis when you feel let down or annoyed. People use different words to mean the same thing and depending upon the intensity of the word—this will have an effect on your confidence. Instead of saying, "I'm enraged about this," say, "I'm a little annoyed." Make a substitute list for the words that you use.

Make sure that they are lower in intensity and then use them. You'll be surprised with the results.

14. Change your "pat" response to a very, everyday general question. For example, when someone asks, "How are you?" change what you normally say. Move away from fine, okay, so-so, I've been better, not so good, etc. Instead come back with something like: wonderful, absolutely terrific, better than fantastic, etc. You get the picture. Then at the end of each day, recall how these responses made an impact on your day.

15. Be appreciative of what you have. Be thankful for what you have in your life right now. Who do you love? Who loves you? Who do you help out? Who helps you out? Think of ways to show your appreciation and then do it.

16. Every morning when you're in the shower, play over in your head the events in the day as though they have already happened and they were a success. Visualize all of the meetings that you had, the people you talked to, the outcomes you had. Visualize success and confidence and it will be so.

17. Improve your body language. The way that you move your body has a massive impact on your confidence levels. Move your body assertively and walk with your head up, shoulders back and as though you've got somewhere very important to go. Feeling low in confidence? Change your body language.

18. Emotion is created by motion. As in seventeen, make sure you

move around consistently. This creates energy and gets the blood pumping around your body; it makes you feel better and more confident. Listen to music that speaks to your soul.

19. Learn to "talk" about yourself. Yes, you heard me! Talk about your achievements and successes more than you currently are. But wisdom dictates that you do not be overbearing. It can be mixed within the topic of conversation. Don't force it, just follow the conversation. The real key here is knowing when enough is enough.

20. And finally, you only live once, so any time that you are down, just ask yourself in 10 or 20 years' time—will what I am worrying about really matter? Don't let today go by without recognizing at least one good thing about your life. Savor that good and make a commitment to yourself to increase that good. You should be a friend to yourself as well as a friend to others. Look around, take a deep breath, and embrace this beautiful day that you have been given. Now, look forward to tomorrow and repeat the process again until you exude in confidence!

Stay in Your Lane

As I sit here feeling a little lost as I sometimes do, I find myself hearing the words of a relative and friend, "Stay in your lane!" He has spoken these words so many, many times over the years that I wasn't even sure if I was hearing them anymore.

But I must have heard them then and even now. Somewhere, deep from my unconscious mind, as I sit with these feelings of wondering which way I should go, what direction my life must take, these words "stay in your lane" burst through loud and clear.

My Lane: now there's a thought to ponder. Over the years, I have tried many things and was quite successful at half of them. However, I found myself pondering over the few things that I was not very successful at. Those were the entrepreneurial ventures that promoted the brand of others. I recalled the sale pitches and the persons involved in the home-based business-type ventures. Most were dedicated enough, nice enough, sincere enough, and they believed in what they were doing. They believed that from it (the venture), they would gain financial independence. But over the years, from one venture to another, the joyfulness and the hopefulness of these entrepreneur exploits would just fizzle out. No one I personally knew became finally independent from these ventures. I heard of those who did, but I didn't know them personally; I just heard about them. So I begin to wonder why did it happen for some and not happen for so many others. After all, they all wanted financial independence.

Many of the companies are still around, with their Representatives and Independent consultants etc., and somebody somewhere has made these ventures work for them, but so many have fallen by the wayside. I happen to be one of them. After some 20-plus years of trying, I finally realized that the home-based business from the standpoint of selling someone else's product or service is just not my lane.

I hate to sit here and think of those years as wasted, trying to succeed in areas that I was never met to embrace. When I think of where I am today and how moving in a direction that "fits" who I am, I see so much progress. Yes, the work is challenging at times, but still, I see results for the efforts I am putting in. I see doors opening and people with similar interests getting involved but not involved the same way that I am. They are bringing to this experience what they are good at; what they are passionate about. It's like a partnership coming together to bring about a fantastic service that will benefit so many people. So why did it take so many years and so many failures for me to come to this conclusion; that I must travel in my lane, go in the direction that was designed for me to go?

I dare say it must have had to do with the "money" factor. It must have been my major motivation. If I were to do this or that and be able to involve 3 to 5 persons more and then they were able to do the same, inside of a few short months, there were to be thousands of dollars rolling into my bank account per month. Yet that "bone on a string" always kept several paces in front of me.

I remember thinking as I would finally shut the door on some of those ventures, it must be nice to be in an environment where you can find the people necessary to make your business and their business thrive. I found myself saying to my sponsors, it must be nice; I am glad it's working for you. But as for me, it's not working and I need to count it as a loss, except for the experience and move on. It took some time, but I learned some valuable lessons.

So now, having moved on, where am I today? Yes, you guessed it, I am traveling "my lane." I was always meant to help and motivate others; by teaching them and encouraging them to become the best they could be by following their path and their destiny, not someone else's.

My best advice that I have learned over the years, which I also take a full dose of on a daily basis, is this; while entrepreneurship is excellent in and of itself, it is not for everyone. It takes hard work, dedication, and a constant and deliberate course of action. The commitment to the success of any business has been a part of your daily existence; always looking for that next person and or opportunity. It's positioning yourself and your brand to be found. Initially, it's like you never really get a vacation. Everyone is not cut out for this sort of thing. I found out that I am not.

So I listen with interest to whoever comes my way with an offer that seems to be working well for them and how I am being solicited to participate. After evaluating the offer from the standpoint of who I am and what I currently do, if it does not fit my lane, I can turn it down. I can no longer run with the packs that are going in the opposite direction. I can't lay down the mantle that I am carrying to pick up another. There are just not that many hours in the day or that much energy in my body (to pursue their goals and mine as well). The same is true for you also.

When you are faced with choices, don't choose an opportunity strictly as a way to make money; choose it because it is your passion. Choose it because you can make it work out for you without your having to change directions and try to become someone you were never met to be.

I am finding out that staying true to my creative side, as I love to write to inspire others, I love to teach and train others. I love directing plays and writing songs. I love developing and planning motivational courses. I love doing research and teaching others about what I have learned. I am a stickler for the factual truths about events, history, the Bible etc. I love coordinating events. I have a flair for public speaking. So I have learned that if what I get involved in does not afford me the opportunity to make use of the gifts that I have, I need to leave it alone.

I have learned that what I do is very important to who I am and that what others do is very important to who they are. When you reach out to work on a business of your own, it must be your own passion. Whether or not you can find three people or five people in order to duplicate yourself should not be the primary goal. You should be doing what you love, what brings you joy and peace of mind. And when you do what you do so well, it will gain the attention of others. The Bible teaches that a man's gift will make room for him and I have seen that principle come alive in my life. In my lane, I can sell what I do because it is who I am. You can do the same. Staying in your lane will enable you to sell what you do because it is who you are! Find your lane and stick with it. It will take you far. Go for it!

For more information, visit http://www.powerup4success.net.

Concentrate on the Prize

Your future is before you. The past is behind you. It's time for a new chapter.

Are you a Trailblazer?

For several years after this award was approved by the Board of Directors of Our Faith-Based Institute of Higher Learning, I thought about being the recipient. I had always been referred to as a self-starter, a branch walker, a person who would step out on twigs, one who finds a way to make things happen even when the odds are against whatever it is, and one who would tackle projects that the likelihood of its success seem near impossible.

So when this award was approved and sanctioned, I looked forward to being a recipient, but that was not the case. For several years I watched and even nominated very deserving individuals and they all walked away with a feeling that I could only imagine. I was happy for everyone who received this prestigious award, but I would be lying if I said I did not want to receive it as well.

As time went on, I began to wonder about my effectiveness in my call. I knew within myself that I took my duties seriously and I worked tirelessly on behalf of others. Often I felt as if no one knew of the work and sacrifices that I was making to get the job done. Sometimes I even wanted to quit, but something inside just wouldn't let me give up on others or myself. I kept going and kept looking for ways to improve the Institute. And somewhere along the way, I forgot about becoming the recipient of that award that I had coveted for so long. I came to a place in my life where I accepted that God was the one who knew all about me and my thoughts and activities, successes, and failures, and I was alright with that.

I lost myself in helping those who wanted more from life and who wanted more from their own experience. I sought out trailblazers. By definition, they are persons who blaze trails for others to follow; they are pathfinders; they are pioneers in a field or an endeavor. I encountered many souls who wanted to achieve more than just an ordinary station in life, and I made it my business to help them in any way that I could. I educated myself and then I educated others. I researched and sought out ways to improve and then taught others to do the same. I used the mediums available to me to communicate to others, words of inspiration. I sought out opportunities to offer others an open door to knowledge and work that would offer personal fulfillment.

Many nights I would come home exhausted, but it was a good exhaustion. I'd fall asleep and rest peacefully. The next day I would walk the track again. And then it happened. I wasn't looking for it; I didn't expect it, and just like that, there it was "The Trailblazer Award." It was presented to me before a packed auditorium, many of whom I knew personally and, of course, many of whom I did not know, but the joy and excitement that filled that room is something I will never forget. I was practically speechless. I don't have the words to describe that moment. It was well worth the wait.

What did I learn from all of this? There is a time and place for everything. The good that you do does get noticed, and eventually, if you do not lose heart, if you keep working and don't get weary if you guard your attitude and stay the course, the reward will come. This particular award speaks to blazing new trails for others to follow; that's what I want to continue to do with my life. What do you want to do with yours? Whatever it is, keep moving towards it, and what is for you will come to you. Don't lose heart. Trailblazer recognition or some other recognition, whatever has your name on it, will eventually come to you if you keep walking that path and doing what is required. Even the Holy Scriptures teach that every man will be rewarded for his deeds, good or bad. Keep focused, stay the course, and your reward will come.

Now you have it. Running has its benefits and its shortfalls. You must determine where you are and what you want to do about it. Just keep in mind while running can be beneficial, this can only be in the short run. You should not let it become a way of life. Challenges and fears have to be faced and dealt with. In the end, it makes life better for you and those you love and helps to fulfill the purpose God created you to accomplish!

My Success Story

My name is Dr. Marci Tilghman Bryant. By profession, I am a teacher and have been employed by both in the public school system and Community College Continuing Education Programs. Currently, I teach in Faith-Based Institutions at the graduate level as well as in the Life Coach Certification Industry. Over the years, I have found my greatest joy comes from helping others reach beyond themselves and/or their circumstances and succeed at something new. I gave very little thought to my own dreams and desires, always esteeming others as more important than myself.

Just over two years ago, a friend of mine gave me a book, Caught Between a Dream and a Job! She stated that when she was window shopping, she saw it and immediately thought of me. She had no idea what the book was about, but she said that the title alone seemed to scream out, "Buy this book for Marci. So she did."

I began reading it right away, and it helped to change my life! My first revelation was that I did have dreams, big dreams, but that I had chosen to let them stay buried because I did not consider them as important as someone else's dreams. Next, the book hit me right between the eyes when it was made clear that I had everything I needed to change my life now. And, third, when I began to evaluate what I had as assets and who I am as a person, I understood that once I developed a plan, I had something to work with already. I had had a plan for years, but for the lack of confidence and encouragement, I let it lie dormant.

I am a writer, yes, I can say it now. I love to write to encourage and inspire others. I am a teacher, yes, I can proclaim that out loud. I love learning and helping others to learn as well. Prior to reading Caught between a Dream and a Job! I felt that all I could ever hope for was a subsidy publishing house and maybe, just maybe, teaching Sunday school at church. You see, all I have ever accomplished I have had to pay my own way, use my own money, borrow from credit cards, and always just seemed to run out of funds when it was time to really promote myself. Money, or the lack thereof, was always a problem.

After reading Caught between a Dream and a Job, I revised my old plan, but this time, with my new attitude. I have value. Inside I believed it but never felt quite confident enough to say it out loud. It's time I acted like I am valuable and went after what I wanted. So I contacted a publisher and went through the process they required in order to be considered as one of their authors. A couple of times, I felt a little nervous and wanted to back out, just run from the uncertainty that lay before me, but now I am glad I did not. After eight weeks of going back and forth through their selection process, I was accepted. For the first time in my life, I got a real publishing contract. This contact would not only publish my work, but they would be instrumental in promoting it as well. I was assigned a team for each step along the process until the book was ready for the general public. I am overwhelmed at the amount of money that was invested from the publisher in order to get my book into the hands of others. I feel grateful and blessed.

Another powerful and stirring motivation entered my spirit by recalling two poignant messages; "Well Able" by Pastor Vincent Harris and "Refreshed, Refueled, and Refired" by Pastor Adrianne Lee. They spoke words that came alive inside of me. They stirred me to action. From Pastor Harris, I left his message believing that I am more than capable of accomplishing great things, but not by running away from challenges but by facing them. Courage is what happens when you face your fear. I accepted that I can do all things through Christ who strengthens me. I don't have to run away from the unknown; after all, I am not facing it alone. The God of Isaac, Abraham, and Jacob is with me in the presence of the Holy Spirit.

Pastor Lee's message was filled to the brim with what one should do to re-invent oneself; that's the Refreshing part: then one must arm oneself with knowledge and wisdom and develop a real plan of action that is in keeping with whom they are meant to be in the earth; that's the Refueling; and lastly, get up and get back out there. Go another round, you've done your homework, reinvested in yourself, and you have everything you need to get the job done. That's being Refired!

I have also taken away some great nuggets from front runners, like the late Zig Ziglar, I am reminded by him that one should "evaluate where you are!" This is so important, after all, you need to know how far you are away from your goal.

John C. Maxwell is another well-read front-runner of mine. If you have not read it, you may want to get a copy of his book, The 21 Indispensable Qualities of a Leader. Among other things, I take away from this book that the power to change how we proceed with our goals in life is really up to us. What we don't have via knowledge, we can get. Many have gone before us and many are walking this path right now; there is help all around us. But the "reach" must come from within. If you don't pursue your dreams, who will? And if not now, when?

Not running away from who I am was one of the best things that I could have ever done for myself. Don't you think it's time that you stopped running too?

Other Books Written by Dr. Bryant:

- In Search of Myself

- Will the Laughter Come Again?

- 101 Ways to Keep Going When the Going Gets Tough (available on Kindle)

Other writing venues: Ezine, Expert Writer

Look for my Christian talk show: "Powerup," on demand at http://www.thenownetwork.org

http://www.lifeandspiritonline.com.

The Voice of One Christian News and Commentary
Visit her page at http://www.authorsden.com

website: http://www.powerup4success.net

ABOUT THE AUTHOR

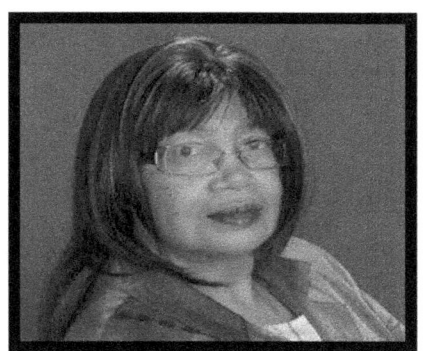

D r. Marci Tilghman-Bryant has been gifted to excel in more than one profession, and to God, she gives the glory. Because of her deep desire to help others succeed, she has maintained a life that has included education and training. She uses that knowledge to develop seminars and workshops to help others grow personally and in the startup of their Christian businesses or ministries. She also teaches at Christian colleges, in some cases, which she helped to establish, and she is a Certified Life Coach Trainer.

She is the senior Pastor of BVT Ministries and the proud mother of two children and eight grandchildren. Additionally, for enjoyment, she writes and directs Christian plays and songs.

You can follow her on Twitter @bryantm100 or connect with her on LinkedIn.

www.ingramcontent.com/pod-product-compliance
Lightning Source LLC
Chambersburg PA
CBHW051549120626
46551CB00013B/1429